PUTTING
THE
PLANET
FIRST

RENEWABLE ENERGY

Nancy Dickmann

WAYLAND
www.waylandbooks.co.uk

First published in Great Britain in 2017
by Wayland

Copyright © Hodder and Stoughton 2017

All rights reserved.

Editors: Paul Mason, Elizabeth Brent
Design: Peter Clayman
ISBN: 978 1 5263 0163 5

10 9 8 7 6 5 4 3 2 1

Wayland, an imprint of
Hachette Children's Group
Part of Hodder and Stoughton
Carmelite House
50 Victoria Embankment
London EC4Y 0DZ

An Hachette UK Company
www.hachette.co.uk
www.hachettechildrens.co.uk

Printed and bound in China

Picture acknowledgements:
All images courtesy of Shutterstock except p7: Getty Images/Kuni Takahashi;
p13: Valeriya Anufriyeva/Shutterstock.com; p26: Getty Images/Arctic-Images.

Every attempt has been made to clear copyright. Should there be any
inadvertent omission, please apply to the publisher for rectification.

The website addresses (URLs) included in this book were valid at the time of
going to press. However, it is possible that contents or addresses may have
changed since the publication of this book. No responsibility for any such
changes can be accepted by either the author or the Publisher.

CONTENTS

WHAT IS RENEWABLE ENERGY?

Your body needs energy to walk, think and kick a ball. Luckily, you don't need to plug yourself in to charge up overnight! Your body gets its energy from the food you eat.

NON-FOOD ENERGY

The gadgets and machines we use are a different story – they do not sit down to lunch and fill up with energy every day! But from smartphones and watches to airplanes and trains, they all have to get their energy from somewhere. Driving to the shops, cooking dinner or sending a text message all use energy, too.

Much of our energy comes from burning fossil fuels: coal, oil or natural gas. Cars burn petrol, which is made from oil. Many cookers and water heaters burn natural gas. Lots of devices use electricity, which is often made by burning coal.

GLOBAL ENERGY USE

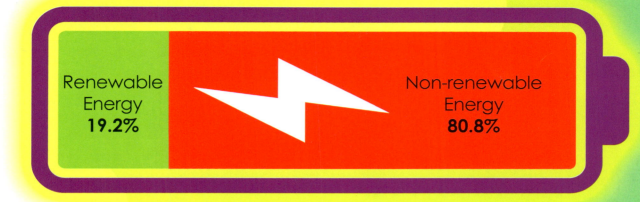

Renewable Energy **19.2%**

Non-renewable Energy **80.8%**

The percentage of renewable energy that we use is increasing, but it is still fairly small.

NON-RENEWABLE AND RENEWABLE

Energy based on burning fossil fuels is called non-renewable. Once a fossil fuel is burned up, it is gone forever. Because fossil fuels took millions of years to form deep underground, if we use up the Earth's supply, there will be no more.

Other types of energy are renewable. They come from things that will never run out, such as sunlight or wind. No matter how much sunlight we harness to generate electricity, there will be more shining down on Earth the next day.

It takes a lot of electricity to power all the lights in big cities, such as Los Angeles, USA.

PROBLEMS WITH FOSSIL FUELS

We burn fossil fuels in our vehicles, and in power stations to generate electricity. Fossil fuels are cheap and efficient, but they also cause problems.

POLLUTION AND GLOBAL WARMING

Burning fossil fuels creates air pollution, which can harm the health of humans, plants and animals. It is also causing global warming. The gases from burning fossil fuels trap heat in the Earth's atmosphere. This is causing the overall temperature of the planet to rise.

Global warming is a big problem, now and for the future. It is causing droughts and more extreme weather, such as hurricanes. To stop global warming, we need to replace fossil fuels with renewable sources of energy.

WORLDWIDE USE OF OIL

1990

2000 +14%

2010 +11%

Every year we use more oil than the year before. In 2000, we used 14 per cent more oil than in 1990. In 2010, we used 11 per cent more oil than in 2000.

Underground coal mines can sometimes catch fire, which releases dangerous gases.

THE RANIGANJ COALFIELDS

Air pollution is not the only problem caused by fossil fuels. Extracting them in the first place can harm the environment.

The Raniganj Coalfield is in India. Miners have tunnelled down below the surface to reach the coal buried there. In places, this has caused the ground above to sink, which is extremely dangerous.

Coal mining is also affecting the local water supply. Water that runs through the mines becomes too polluted to drink. Even so, many local people rely on the streams and rivers for bathing and drinking. They have no choice but to use water that is not safe.

WIND POWER

Winds blow across the Earth's surface every day. They are unlikely to ever stop blowing, so wind is a renewable energy source.

WIND TO ELECTRICITY

Today, wind energy is often used to generate electricity. When wind blows, it turns the blades of a large windmill, called a turbine. Inside the turbine, a generator converts the spinning motion into electricity. The electricity can then be sent though wires to wherever it is needed.

Giant wind turbines are becoming a common sight in the countryside and in the sea, close to the coast. Often, many turbines are built in the same area, forming a wind farm.

WIND ENERGY PRODUCTION PER PERSON

Key:
50 megawatts (MW)

Denmark
751 MW

Spain
485 MW

Portugal
420 MW

UK
134 MW

 Denmark produces more wind energy per person than any other country in the world.

Wind power can bring electricity to many people who have never had it before.

SMALL-SCALE WIND POWER

In towns and cities, wires connect homes to a system called a power grid. The grid transports electricity. But there is no grid in some rural areas, so the people there can't connect their homes. They need a different source of electricity.

Gurugoda is a tiny village in Sri Lanka that doesn't have access to a power grid. Until recently, Gurugoda's residents did not have electricity in their homes. Then a wind turbine was installed in the village. The turbine is only small, but it provides enough electricity for 13 homes. Thanks to wind power, the residents of Gurugoda can now have electric lights, and power for televisions and radios.

OFFSHORE WIND

Winds are stronger and more frequent over the oceans. To harness their energy, engineers have started building wind farms out at sea. There are already more than 3,000 turbines installed off Europe's coasts, with more added every year.

CHALLENGES

Building large offshore turbines in deep water is a massive challenge. Because of this, most are built where the water is less than 50 metres deep. This makes them much easier to construct.

ADVANTAGES

On land, people often don't like the way that wind turbines look. This is not a problem when they're offshore and out of sight. There is also more space available out at sea.

Offshore wind turbines are huge structures.

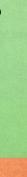

House	Small turbine	Statue of Liberty	Offshore turbine
about **8 m**	**17 m**	**93 m**	**200 m**

ANHOLT WIND FARM

Anholt Wind Farm in Denmark is one of the world's largest offshore wind farms. It was built in 2012 and 2013, in the shallow waters between Denmark and Sweden. There are 111 turbines in an area about the size of the Welsh city of Cardiff. Each turbine is the height of a 40-storey building, and each blade is half as long as a football pitch!

Working together, the turbines at Anholt can produce about 400 megawatts of electricity when the wind is blowing strongly. When the winds are low, they produce less. Even then, though, Anholt generates enough electricity to power nearly 300,000 homes.

Anholt Wind Farm is built in an area where the water is less than 20 metres deep.

SOLAR ELECTRICITY

The energy in sunlight dries our clothes and helps plants to grow, but it can also be used in other ways. Photovoltaic ('PV' for short) panels capture the sun's energy and turn it into electricity.

You may have seen small PV panels on a calculator. They come in lots of different sizes. Some people use small PVs to charge their phones in remote places. Bigger PVs can be installed on most rooftops. And in some places, 'solar farms' of thousands of panels generate electricity for the power grid. A large solar farm can produce enough electricity to power tens of thousands of homes.

WORLDWIDE SOLAR PV CAPACITY

The amount of energy we generate from solar power is growing quickly.

2010
40 gigawatts

2006
7 gigawatts

2016
310 gigawatts

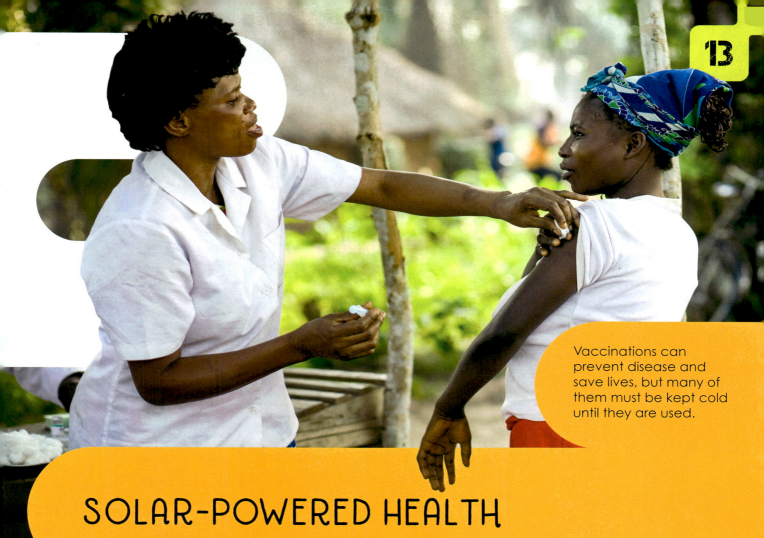

Vaccinations can prevent disease and save lives, but many of them must be kept cold until they are used.

SOLAR-POWERED HEALTH

In Ghana, many remote communities don't have access to the power grid. This affects medical care. Doctors and nurses need electricity to keep medicines refrigerated, and to power equipment for health tests. Some clinics use diesel-powered generators, but these are noisy and create pollution.

Now Ghana's health service is starting to use mobile clinics with solar panels built into the roof. The electricity produced by the panels can power medical equipment. It also charges batteries that store the electrical energy. This makes it possible to keep the medicine fridge running at night, when the sun is down.

SOLAR HEATING

Not all solar panels produce electricity. Some types of panel collect the sun's heat and use it to provide people's homes with hot water.

SOLAR HEAT COLLECTORS

Solar heat collectors have tubes inside filled with thick fluid. The sun warms up the fluid, and the hot fluid is used to heat water.

In an average house, about 18 per cent of the energy used is for heating water. Many homes get their hot water from a boiler that uses natural gas – a polluting fossil fuel. Using the sun's heat does not cause pollution, so it is better for the environment. It is also free, so by using solar heating, families can save a lot of money.

In 2009, human energy use (shown by the tiny red sun) was 0.07 per cent of the amount produced by the sun.

If a home's solar panels produce more electricity than it uses, the owners can sell the extra electricity back to the grid.

AUSTRALIAN SOLAR POWER

Installing solar panels on your house is expensive. Even in a sunny country such as Australia it can take 10 years to pay back the cost of the panels. As a result, few Australians used to install them.

Then, in 2008, the government started helping people to pay for solar panels. The programme was extremely popular, and now 20 per cent of Australian homes have solar panels. In some areas, up to 40 per cent of homes have them. This has helped Australia to reduce its use of fossil fuels.

ELECTRICITY FROM WATER

Wind is not the only thing that can spin a turbine to generate electricity. The energy of flowing water in rivers can also be harvested using turbines.

HYDROELECTRIC DAMS

The energy from flowing water is called hydroelectric power ('hydro' means 'to do with water'). The turbines are usually part of a dam that blocks a river. The dam builds up a store of water behind it, which can be released when it is needed. Engineers can let more water through when more electricity needs to be generated. Once the water is through the turbines, it continues down the river towards the sea.

Each one of the Itaipu Dam's 20 turbines could power a city of 1.5 million people on its own.

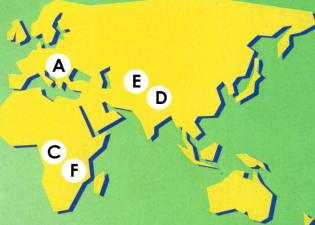

Fifteen countries get three-quarters or more of their electricity from hydroelectric schemes. This map shows the top six, and the percentage of their power that comes from hydroelectricity.

A =1. Albania 100%
B =1. Paraguay 100%
C =3. DR Congo 99%
D =3. Nepal 99%
E =3. Tajikistan 99%
F =3. Zambia 99%

DAM POWER

The Itaipu Dam is the world's second-largest power plant. Only the Three Gorges Dam in China is bigger.

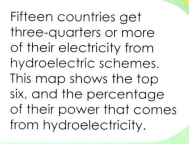

The Itaipu Dam first opened in 1984. It is located on the Paraná River, which forms part of the border between Brazil and Paraguay. The two countries cooperated to build the enormous structure, which is as tall as a 65-storey building.

Inside the dam are 20 large turbines. Between them, these turbines can produce about 15 per cent of all the energy used in Brazil, and about 75 per cent of Paraguay's energy.

WAVE POWER

Ocean waves contain a huge amount of energy, but engineers are still working out the best way of capturing this and turning it into electricity.

ELECTRICITY FROM WAVES

Some long, thin wave-power machines ride on the surface of the water. The different sections are connected, like the carriages on a train. As a wave moves past, the 'carriages' move up and down. This motion is turned into electricity, which is sent through wires to the shore.

Other devices – such as LIMPET, on page 19 – use the power of waves to force air into a cylinder. This compressed air drives a turbine, producing electricity.

ELECTRICITY PRODUCTION BY WAVE SIZE

Small wave

Can run 15 washing machines

Medium wave

Can run 50 washing machines

Large wave

Can run 70 washing machines

Even a small wave crashes against the shore with tremendous power.

LIMPET

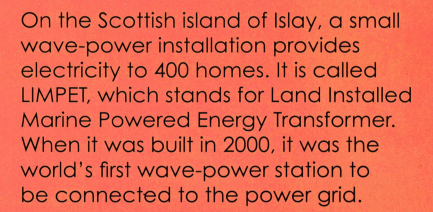

On the Scottish island of Islay, a small wave-power installation provides electricity to 400 homes. It is called LIMPET, which stands for Land Installed Marine Powered Energy Transformer. When it was built in 2000, it was the world's first wave-power station to be connected to the power grid.

LIMPET uses a type of wave-power machine called an oscillating water column. A hollow chamber on the coast fills with water when a wave hits the shore. This pushes air out of the chamber, and the force of the moving air spins a turbine to generate electricity.

USING THE TIDES

If you've ever spent time at the beach, you'll know that the tide comes in and goes out twice each day. When this happens, huge amounts of water move.

It is possible to install turbines to capture some of the tide's energy. Tidal power stations are often built in bays, or in estuaries, where a river meets the sea.

The power stations usually have a long, low dam, called a barrage. The barrage lets water in at high tide. When the tide goes out, the water flows out through gates in the barrage. Turbines in the gates spin as the water flows past, generating electricity.

GOOD LOCATIONS FOR TIDAL POWER STATIONS

Some countries could get lots of electricity from tidal power.

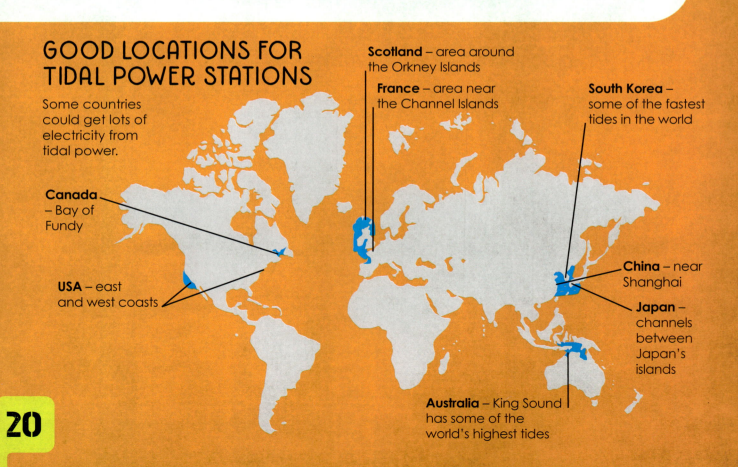

Scotland – area around the Orkney Islands

France – area near the Channel Islands

South Korea – some of the fastest tides in the world

Canada – Bay of Fundy

USA – east and west coasts

China – near Shanghai

Japan – channels between Japan's islands

Australia – King Sound has some of the world's highest tides

A tidal barrage can upset the delicate balance of plant and animal life on the coast. It may lead to there being fewer fish for birds to catch.

SIHWA LAKE POWER STATION

The world's largest tidal power station is in South Korea. It is located where Gyeonggi Bay meets the Yellow Sea.

A long tidal barrage stretches for about 13 kilometres across the opening of the bay. Inside are 10 turbines. Whether the tides flow in or out, the water rushing past the turbines generates electricity.

The power station took seven years to build, but since it started operating in 2011, it has produced a huge amount of electricity, reducing South Korea's use of fossil fuels. It has been so successful that the government is planning more tidal power stations for other locations.

HEAT FROM UNDERGROUND

The Earth is hot below the surface and the deeper you dig, the hotter it gets. The temperatures under the crust are high enough to melt rock. This heat can be used by humans.

Molten rock (called magma) rises and collects just below the planet's crust. It heats up any water that is trapped underground. We can tap into this hot water, and pipe it into homes to keep them warm.

In some places, the underground water is so hot it has turned to steam. We can bring the steam to the surface, too, then use it to spin turbines and generate electricity. Heat from the Earth is known as geothermal energy.

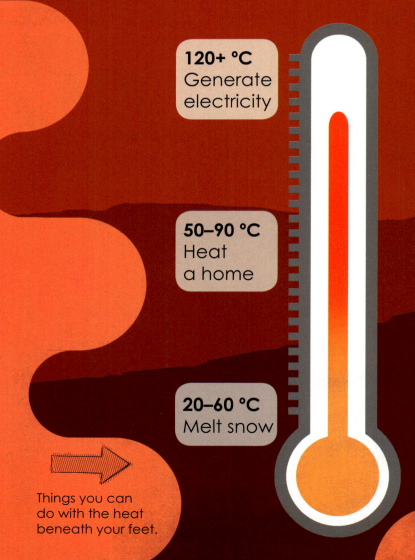

120+ °C Generate electricity

50–90 °C Heat a home

20–60 °C Melt snow

Things you can do with the heat beneath your feet.

In Iceland, greenhouses heated by geothermal power are used to grow fruits, vegetables and flowers.

HEATED ROADS

Iceland is dotted with volcanoes, geysers and natural hot springs, so is the perfect place for using geothermal energy. About 25 per cent of Iceland's electricity comes from geothermal energy.

Iceland is cold for much of the year, and most homes use geothermal water for heating. There is so much free heat that many people do not even have double-glazed windows.

Iceland gets a lot of snow in winter. Beneath the snowy streets and pavements of the capital city, Reykjavik, there are networks of pipes. Geothermal water flows through them and melts the snow. This is better for the environment than driving snowploughs through the city.

BIOMASS ENERGY

If you have ever built a camp-fire, then you have used biomass energy. Biomass is any substance made from living things – usually plants – that can be burned as a fuel.

Plants use the energy in sunlight to make their own food. Burning the plant releases that energy. After the plant has been harvested, farmers can grow more, so biomass is renewable. We can use biomass energy to cook, generate electricity and power vehicles.

The plants are not always simply burnt. Maize, soybeans and other crops can be turned into liquid fuels, such as ethanol or biodiesel. These fuels can be used instead of petrol or diesel in cars and other vehicles.

IN A YEAR:

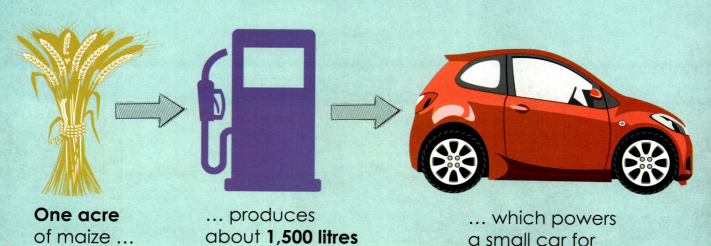

One acre of maize …

… produces about **1,500 litres** of ethanol …

… which powers a small car for about **32,000 km.**

24

There are more than 8,000 biogas plants like this one in Germany.

ELECTRICITY FROM BACTERIA

In Bavaria, Germany, a power plant is using mouldy old food to produce bio-electricity.

When we throw away food waste, tiny living things called bacteria start to break it down. This process produces a gas, usually called 'biogas'. A biogas plant in Bavaria collects food waste from factories, then puts it into a machine called a digester. The digester captures the biogas, which is then burned to generate electricity.

When the food waste is broken down, a substance called digestate is left behind. The digestate is full of nutrients, so it is used as fertiliser on farmers' fields.

HYDROGEN FUEL CELLS

What if we could find a fuel that was renewable and caused no pollution? It sounds too good to be true, but a device called a hydrogen fuel cell can do just that.

In a hydrogen fuel cell, hydrogen and oxygen from the air are combined. This produces electricity, and the only waste product is water.

THE HIDDEN COST OF HYDROGEN

There is a problem with hydrogen fuel cells, namely how the hydrogen is produced in the first place. Most hydrogen is made from natural gas, which is a fossil fuel. So until scientists can develop a clean, cheap and renewable way of producing hydrogen, hydrogen fuel cell vehicles probably will not be a common sight.

HYDROGEN FUEL CELLS IN ACTION

A fuel cell needs hydrogen, and oxygen from the air, in order to produce electricity.

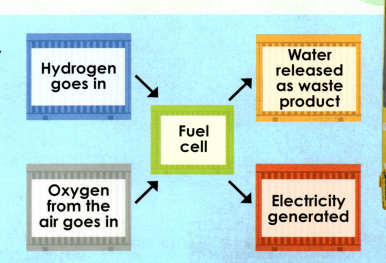

Hydrogen goes in → Fuel cell → Water released as waste product

Oxygen from the air goes in → Fuel cell → Electricity generated

26

HYDROGEN BUSES

The air in busy city centres is often polluted, because of all the cars and buses that drive through each day. The problem is usually worst when people are going to or from work.

The city of Aberdeen, in Scotland, has a fleet of 10 buses that run on hydrogen fuel cells. There is a refuelling station at one of their bus depots, and hydrogen fuel is produced there for the buses to use. The buses can carry lots of passengers: an average of 37,000 people every month. Because they emit only water vapour, the hydrogen fuel cell buses help to reduce Aberdeen's pollution.

Buses that run on hydrogen fuel cells look a lot like regular buses.

THE FUTURE

At some point in the future, renewable energy will be the main source of electricity around the world. In the United States, for example, it could be providing 80 per cent of electricity by 2050.

CARS AND TRANSPORT

One big challenge is finding a renewable replacement for the oil that fuels our vehicles. Electric cars are becoming more common. At the moment, the electricity they use is unlikely to come from renewable sources. If this changes, it will make a big difference to the world.

NEW TECHNOLOGIES

Scientists will keep finding new ways of generating renewable energy. Wave power, in particular, has not yet been fully developed. If we can find a good way to harness the power of waves, they will provide large amounts of renewable energy.

Scientists predict that worldwide energy use will rise in the future, and the percentage of it provided by renewable energy will also go up.

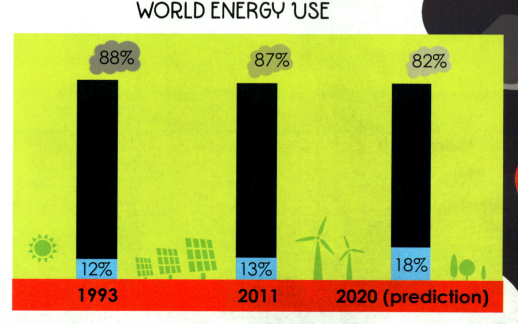

WORLD ENERGY USE

- ■ non-renewable
- ■ renewable

1993	2011	2020 (prediction)
88%	87%	82%
12%	13%	18%

Geothermal power is provided by the same underground heat that created Costa Rica's volcanoes.

A RENEWABLE COUNTRY

In 2015, the Central American country of Costa Rica set a world record: for 75 days in a row, all of its electricity came from renewable sources. In total, there were 285 days in 2015 when the country used only renewable energy for electricity.

Costa Rica gets a lot of its electricity from hydropower, and also uses geothermal, solar and wind power. People in Costa Rica still use petrol and diesel to fuel cars and buses, so the country never runs completely fossil-fuel free. But their achievement is a good example of the possibilities of renewable energy.

GLOSSARY

barrage long, low dam built across a body of water

biomass plant or animal matter, such as wood or manure, which can be used as fuel

dam wall built across a river or stream to create a pond or lake

energy the ability to do work; energy can take many different forms

estuary wide area at the end of a river, where it meets the sea

fossil fuels oil, coal and natural gas, which began to be formed from the remains of living things, millions of years ago

fuel anything such as wood or oil that can be burned as a source of energy

generator machine that turns motion into electrical energy

geothermal energy energy generated from the heat below ground

geyser natural spring that occasionally shoots a stream of hot water or steam into the air

global warming the increase in the Earth's average temperature

hydroelectric power electricity generated by moving water

natural gas mixture of gases found in the Earth's crust that can be burned as a fuel

oil thick liquid found beneath the Earth's surface that can be burned for fuel; it is often called petroleum or crude oil

pollution when a substance is released and has harmful effects

power grid network of power stations and wires that carry electricity to where it is needed

renewable able to be renewed instead of running out

solar panel a flat device that either captures sunlight and turns it into electricity, or uses the sun's energy to heat water

tide regular change in the height of the surface of the oceans

turbine machine with rotating blades

FINDING OUT MORE

WEBSITES

At the Children's University, you can find out more about renewable and non-renewable energy on this fun website: www.childrensuniversity.manchester.ac.uk/interactives/science/energy/renewable

The US Energy Information Administration website has a lot of information about different types of renewable energy: www.eia.gov/kids/energy.cfm?page=renewable_home-basics

The British government has a web-based activity for seeing how you can reduce your energy usage: my2050.decc.gov.uk

FURTHER READING

Let's Discuss Energy Resources: Wind Power
by Richard and Louise Spilsbury (Wayland, 2010)

Earth Debates: How Harmful Are Fossil Fuels?
by Catherine Chambers (Heinemann Educational Books, 2015)

Eco Works: How Renewable Energy Works
by Geoff Barker (Franklin Watts, 2015)

Source to Resource: Solar:
From Sunshine to Light Bulb
by Michael Bright (Wayland, 2016)

INDEX